Pitching for Lawyers

Using Marketing Communications Techniques to Improve your Win Ratio

Author
Rebecca Harding

Managing director
Sian O'Neill

Pitching for Lawyers: Using Marketing Communications Techniques to Improve your Win Ratio
is published by

Globe Law and Business Ltd
3 Mylor Close
Horsell
Woking
Surrey GU21 4DD
United Kingdom
Tel: +44 20 3745 4770
www.globelawandbusiness.com

Pitching for Lawyers: Using Marketing Communications Techniques to Improve your Win Ratio

ISBN 9781787422742
EPUB ISBN 9781787422759
Adobe PDF ISBN 9781787422766
Mobi ISBN 9781787422773

Table of contents

Acknowledgements

Thank you to all my kind friends, business colleagues and lawyers around the world – from New Zealand to New York and Leicester – who have helped me with this. I could never have produced this without your experiences, encouragement and support.

And thank you to the lovely Sian O'Neill from Globe Law and Business for trusting me with this project.

But most of all, I have to mention my very patient children, who have had to wait quietly while I wrote and edited, and forgave me when I was sometimes late making their dinner.

I. Introduction

1. Getting started

This special report is designed to help you in all sorts of pitching situations – in other words, when you are presenting yourself and your work in a favourable way to a target client or contact, with the intention of winning or retaining work.

The issues discussed and the process you are taken through are just as applicable whether you are:

- meeting a new prospect;
- having lunch with a contact;
- working with existing clients;
- writing a proposal document for a new client;
- putting together a response to a request for proposal (RFP);
- presenting to a business; or
- making a speech publicly to a cohesive group, which may lead to work.

Throughout this text, there are short case studies and thoughts from lawyers, accountants and business people. Of those who contributed, 99% wished to remain anonymous and so all references are anonymous.

The bottom line is that you are always pitching and this tends to be something that you learn on the job. Some people are very good at this naturally and have an instinctive feel for what appeals to others. Many professionals, however, receive little or no help on how to approach pitching. You are supposed to be born with a genetic predisposition to effective pitching!

> A Russian lawyer says: "It's the meeting, pitching and winning that's so hard. Doing the job is easy!"

Winning is hard and sometimes we need to be a little kinder to ourselves in our expectations. Many people feel a subconscious sense of desperation when approaching pitches, believing that they must pitch for absolutely every opportunity that presents itself and win at all costs. Often this is driven by demanding targets. By being kinder to ourselves, we are not giving up on ambition; we are being realistic about what is possible. It also means improving what we are doing in order to increase our chances of winning when the odds are stacked more favourably.

> "I dropped into the office for a coffee and they came and sat round the table. They then told me they had a proposal to put together and asked me would I do for them. I asked what it was and they told me that it was for a multimillion-pound global project. 'Wow,' I said, 'that's brilliant. When do you need it for?' A couple of them giggled nervously. 'The day after tomorrow. Is that okay?' 'How much have you done?' I asked. A couple of them giggled again. 'Nothing,' they said and grinned sheepishly."

Many people find pitching stressful, difficult and pressured, whether it is a one-to-one meeting or a formal presentation. As a result, many lawyers confess that they end up leaving it to the last minute. They then end up rushing and it becomes a cut-and-paste exercise, butchering the material from a previous pitch. The team end up putting pressure on one another, everyone gets stressed and frustrated, and the errors creep in.

> "When I first met my potential new accountant, I was disappointed to realise that he had done no research about my business, what I did or who I was. The meeting ended up with me giving him advice on how to win new clients. He then sent me a proposal document, which was obviously a standard piece of work that he used with everybody. Some of it was simply not applicable to me; some of it read strangely as it had been edited so many times; and my name was wrong in some places and the previous client's details were still included in others."

"By being kinder to ourselves, we are not giving up on ambition; we are being realistic about what is possible. It also means improving what we are doing in order to increase our chances of winning."

The fundamentals of the method and the thought process in this report are the key. Professionalism within the pitching process gives clients a strong indication of the quality of both the work and the relationship they are likely to have with you.

What all in-house lawyers and business people are clear about are the common problems that they experience when lawyers pitch to them in a variety of situations. This report is built around their feedback and analysis, and addresses these issues.

Some of the big accounting firms have advanced pitching departments organised around winning audits. We can learn some lessons here. They must work hard at differentiating themselves from other large accountancy firms in providing a product. Whether we are big or small, the things that are different about us and how those will benefit the client are just as important.

The most important professional skill you have is that of listening. Listening to your client, listening to the marketplace, listening to your prospects and genuinely understanding things from their point of view are the keys to all selling. You must understand their needs and problems, not what you want to sell them. Then you can tailor a product or a service so it works for your client.

"Whether we are big or small, the things that are different about us and how those will benefit the client are just as important."

We have all stood at a drinks party where we are talking about ourselves and then we suddenly realise that the person we are talking to has completely glazed over. They have already talked to a whole bunch of other people, all going on about themselves. So you finish what you are saying and ask a question about them. Suddenly, you have engaged their interest. Pitching is exactly the same. We need to be sensitive to the target client's reactions and avoid them glazing over at all costs. We must keep them engaged and interested. This is always going to be hard because they have had the same conversation with six other people before us. We need to think about what will make us different and more interesting than the others.

It's important to think about an RFP, or any type of proposal document or pitch, in a completely different way. It isn't about you. It's about sorting out a whole bunch of problems for your client. What you are trying to do is give them the information they need to make a decision.

"If you were replaced tomorrow, what would the world lose?"

We all avoid things when we don't know where to start. The process set out here should give you confidence to approach pitches with some sort of structure and a methodology that you can manage and feel in control of. It should help to take away some of the unpredictability within the pitching journey.

2. Using this report

Every pitching situation differs and sometimes you will not be able to find out all the information you need to apply all aspects of the methodology set out here – a lunch meeting and a formal presentation are very different. However, if you do not follow the process in its entirety, it does not mean that it is not worthwhile using any of it. Although this report takes you through an entire process, aspects can be used alone or in combination, depending on the situation you are approaching and what you need to do. Employing some of these methods will drastically improve your approach and you will present yourself to your client far more effectively.

The report is designed to support lawyers of all levels, with varied experience of pitching to potential clients. It will help young lawyers starting out, as well as refining the skills of those who are highly experienced in winning business.

You may already be doing a number of the things covered in this report or some points may seem obvious to you. If this is the case, focus on those areas where you can improve and build them into what you are already doing.

II. Where we are now

1. Where do the opportunities come from?

Firms adopt a variety of methods for targeting and identifying potential clients, just as we do as professional individuals. Some have a formalised programme over a long period of time using a sophisticated client relationship management system; others have target businesses identified through analysis of the market locally or nationally, depending on the size of firm. Many do not and leave it up to the individual lawyers to build contacts and networks, and target clients. It is always preferable for a firm to have a coordinated programme, share knowledge and work towards strategic targets which fit with business objectives. This is likely to enhance its success rate, as well as making lawyers feel supported in reaching their personal targets.

Trying to get on the tender list for bigger businesses can be a challenge. Branding, marketplace recognition and contacts are a strong advantage here. Asking directly can be highly successful!

As individuals, people are often afraid to ask for referrals from contacts and clients, but this is often the best way to build new relationships that can lead to work. After all, your credibility is already established with the new contact through your referrer. Stop and look at all the people you know, and you could be pleasantly surprised.

We all meet people at professional events and ask for follow-up lunches, meetings or coffee in the hope of building a connection strong enough to lead to work. The problem with many of these networking events is that they are packed with lawyers and accountants, and the number of actual businesses is few. Building expertise in niche industries or in particular technical areas can open doors to new types of networking opportunities. Social interactions, associations and clubs can be productive. One thing is clear: it is a time-consuming process and takes investment in terms of thought and care over the long term.

In all these cases, much of the work goes into the initial contact, but during the process of securing the actual work, something is lost. We begin to talk about ourselves; we don't have time to research; we hope our personalities will carry us through. We delegate to someone else and ask them to put information material together for the meeting. They end up cutting and pasting old material into new with little knowledge of who it is for.

Maybe we can do better. Maybe if we did do better, we could move ahead of the competition and shine in the marketplace.

2. International pitching

Finding opportunities to pitch for business internationally in order to build international credentials and experience has become increasingly crucial for law firms of all sizes. The fear is that firms without this experience will be left behind the rest of the market and will be unable to compete in the coming years.

The pace of change in the global business landscape is rapid. Enhanced digital platforms and the speed of technological developments are now allowing businesses to conduct activities in many different countries with ease. Many of those countries, such as the United Kingdom, have introduced measures, support and encouragement to help businesses of all sizes 'go global'.

World Trade Organization (WTO) figures show that worldwide, 60% of the largest small and medium-sized enterprises (SMEs) are already doing business overseas; and even among so-called micro-companies, around 10% now have international business too. The growth of e-commerce and communications platforms is driving those percentages higher each and every day. WTO data shows that among internet-enabled SMEs – that is, companies with the systems in place to access and service clients online – the percentage that do business abroad is close to 100%.

For those that are not already part of a global firm, gaining international experience and access to international markets is achieved by merging with firms abroad or by joining international legal networks such as Legalink and Interlaw.

However, partners are still not managing to pitch internationally with firms within their network. They are encountering a number of issues, which are not being successfully dealt with on a practical basis. Many of these issues also affect the overseas offices of bigger firms when they try to work together on cross-border cases.

Table 1. Issues affecting international pitching

Issues affecting international pitching	Comment
Lack of relationships between offices of different nationalities and a resulting lack of confidence	Often the relationship within an international network is left to one individual lawyer who is interested and enthusiastic. This is tokenism. Without investment in international relationships from lawyers throughout your own firm, trust and confidence in working together will always be low.
Joint branded materials	Particularly within some of the smaller international networks, there is a lack of investment in joint pitching materials and resources that would provide consistency of approach and could be accessed quickly and efficiently by the group.
• Consistency of approach • Pitch lead and coordination	Ironing out a consistent approach to pitching not only means that you can be more efficient, but also ensures quality and that clients receive the same standards and experience wherever they are. This has an impact on your network's brand and reflects on the work that you are likely to do for clients. It is essential that everyone knows their role within the pitch process and who will lead. Developing a system or framework for this will ensure clarity for all.
Capturing capabilities and credentials	Capturing capabilities and credentials across different international offices takes a lot of time and work, but once it is done, it is a valuable resource. It is also a good idea to have a number of well-written case studies that can demonstrate what your network is capable of. The issue here is finding someone who is prepared to lead the project. Investing in outside support would be wise. This process is also useful in identifying synergies between offices and potential opportunities. It may also provide ideas for specific new services.

continued on next page

Table 1. Issues affecting international pitching *Continued*

Issues affecting international pitching	Comment
• Fees and homogenous billing • Terms and conditions	These practical issues must be thrashed out before pitching for work. The client will want a simplistic approach that is easy to comprehend. Business does not want unnecessary complications with a variety of terms, conditions and fees for different countries.
• Delivery and lead on transaction • Communication channels with the client • Common and consistent reporting mechanisms	It is essential to have an established framework for client delivery when involved in cross-border work within your network. Once again, spending time dealing with these issues in advance of any work, rather than during the project, is time well invested and will affect and enhance your reputation in the long term. It is not only important to ensure that your client work is conducted well. In order for the network to successfully pitch together, people must feel they are capable of delivering together at a high standard and this knowledge in itself will breed confidence.

The firms or networks that manage to crack these issues and solve them will be able to take a leading position in the international marketplace. Currently, SMEs globally have little legal choice. They do not want to use the big firms because they are too expensive and too large for their needs. Some of the mid-tier firms are not performing as well as they might because of the issues listed above, despite having one brand and overseas offices of their own. They are still expensive. The firms that are part of legal networks all have very different ideas, aims and objectives of how they want to use their network and what they want out of it. Without a cohesive and consolidated strategy, the firms within these networks are unlikely to be able to pitch together successfully on an international basis. The market is wide open.

3. Types of pitches

Pitches come in all sorts of shapes and sizes. They don't have to be formalised; sometimes they can be in very relaxed and casual situations. The skills you use will be the same for all and preparation is essential.

3.1 From the coffee...

We meet people for coffee in order to get to know them. Everyone understands the subtext: we are looking to explore mutually beneficial opportunities. The fact is, we are all like travelling salesmen and we want to put out our wares; it's just that they are not watches! Equally, other people want to sell to you.

What is amazing, though, is the number of people who turn up knowing absolutely nothing about the person they are meeting.

> "They often don't bother to look online. One lawyer never noticed that I'd actually worked for their firm some years earlier. I was on their alumni list and I received information from them regularly. I knew all about them, but he had failed to find out about me. And this would have been a good point of connection between us for the meeting."

A little research can make a huge difference in establishing a relationship. These days, there is no excuse not to do research when Google or LinkedIn can do so much of the work for you.

> "A few months ago, I was running an exploratory meeting in order to write a report. The lawyers who were attending the meeting were not sure how the meeting was going to run. One came in and I could see he was somewhat uncomfortable. He said, 'Are you going to start questioning me, then?' 'Yes,' I

"Pitches come in all sorts of shapes and sizes. They don't have to be formalised; sometimes they can be in very relaxed and casual situations. The skills you use will be the same for all and preparation is essential."

replied. 'I have some very serious questions for you'. He frowned. 'So,' I said, 'tell me what it was like being a tennis pro.' The atmosphere in the room changed instantly: he was chuffed that I knew, taken aback that I had done so much research on him and very happy to talk about something he loved. Through a very simple piece of research, a relationship was created and I was able to differentiate myself as a professional in his mind."

3.2 ...To the request for proposal or tender

Clients do not always get it right. We have all seen some absolutely terrible RFPs that make no sense and do not include half the information required in order to respond. Sometimes you are presented with ridiculous timescales, which will put your team under far too much pressure. You need to decide whether trying to do these RFPs is realistic or sensible. Perhaps you are just being asked to pitch so that they can see who is out there and compare them to the incumbent law firm. If you decide to respond, researching the client and their needs is essential. They are individuals too and they want to know that you have found out as much about them and their firm as possible.

> "Clients judge you on the quality of your advice and the depth of your care and understanding of them, whether you give it over coffee or in a formal presentation. The point is, you're talking about them and their problems."

Whether you are talking to individuals or responding to an RFP, if you understand the business and its problems, and listen, you will be able to present your own services, ideas and work in a way that appeals directly to your target client. Working out where that appeal lies is the key behind successful pitching.

> "The proposal was a super-thoughtful analysis, which showed me that they understood my firm, my needs and my stakeholders. They presented it to me at a good time, making me think about things that I had not thought about. It demonstrated both their legal expertise and their understanding of the business and sector."

4. Win ratios

Gauging the percentage of pitches you have won is useful in determining your current success rate and then working out whether you are improving by introducing a new approach. It does not have to be a scientifically accurate figure; having a rough idea of how you are doing is adequate. The usual success rate for law firms is about 30%, but some firms have reached up to 80% by changing their methods and thinking differently about the process. This figure includes any more formalised meeting where you are trying to win business.

"Gauging the percentage of pitches you have won is useful in determining your current success rate and then working out whether you are improving by introducing a new approach."

5. Where do people go wrong when pitching?

The head of global operations for a large private equity company said that lawyers often don't check out the background of the organisation in enough depth. For example, he wanted them to know about all the transactions his private equity company had conducted over the last year. He expected them to know where he had worked before and the fact that his old firm had a new chief executive. These details showed him that the lawyers were market aware and paid attention to detail. He wanted to see full experience and credentials. He said that many lawyers did not understand their clients' motivations. Simply by checking whether the business was privately owned rather than publicly quoted, the lawyers could change their approach. Cash flow alone would be the equity company's big motivator, not share price. He said that surprisingly, many failed to do this and so made proposals that were not framed in the right way. He wanted to see a client-centric pitch structured around his interests. Lawyers often presented him with an M&A proposal and 'one-off' fees for this, together with proposals and fees for other ongoing work. When he considered these fees, he always looked at them in relation to exit multiples. Every cost would be 'cost x10' before they exited the business and

> every benefit would be 'benefit x10' too. He did not want to spend money unless he could see the 'x10 benefit' or the potential increase in value. Lawyers rarely brought him this.
>
> One in-house counsel said that the biggest problem was the fact that the legal firms didn't see the client, the client's team or the client's business in context or as having longer-term objectives. He said they did not see it as a relationship, but instead saw the work simply as spasmodic, isolated transactions. He wanted proactive, regular and thoughtful contact with the law firm to build real understanding and spot opportunities across a number of areas within their legal services provision. He also felt that in-house issues arise in context and are rarely shaped to fit neatly into a law firm departmental specialism. He believed this was an opportunity for the law firm to cross-sell, but instead it often became a negligence issue where the pitching partner missed something essential because it was outside their core competencies.

Fortunately, there are some very common mistakes that people make and businesses are clear about the areas where law firms need to improve. This makes it much easier for us to start putting them right! Getting feedback whether you win or lose is essential. People are generally very fair and will compliment you on what you have done successfully, as well as helping you to identify constructive areas for improvement.

It is important to remember that while you may be familiar with the pitching standards for your own and other law firms, you may not have seen the quality of pitches that your target clients are being exposed to from other industries and suppliers. Some markets support highly sophisticated pitching techniques. So your own pitch will be judged not only in relation to the other law firms you are competing with, but also in relation to other supplier interactions, including proposals, presentations and meetings. It is important to take note of how other businesses approach the process of winning work.

> Another in-house lawyer said he had invited a firm to present him with a plan of where they thought work and challenges for the in-house team would arise over the forthcoming financial year and how they might help him. He wanted this presented far enough ahead that he could include their ideas in his budget submissions for the financial year. The law firm successfully provided a document which analysed the company's sector, the company and the team. They put together a good SWOT analysis of where he might need their external advice and

support, as well as explaining why and giving him suggestions for the next steps to take. However, the relationship partner, who arrived to present the paper to the in-house counsel, had clearly not read the document, had not thought through the content and had not brought any other relevant colleagues. He did not explain any areas other than his own and failed to suggest an action plan to move forward. As a result, the in-house counsel used the insight from the proposal document, but worked with another firm. He thought that if the relationship partner couldn't be bothered – regardless of how much work was being done by others in the background – then it was unlikely to be an effective relationship.

Businesses' common complaints about legal pitches – whether in meetings, proposals for work or responses to RFPs – are set out in Table 2.

"It is important to remember that while you may be familiar with the pitching standards for your own and other law firms, you may not have seen the quality of pitches that your target clients are being exposed to from other industries and suppliers."

Table 2. Common mistakes

Common mistakes	How to avoid them
Not answering the question	It is easy to cut and paste an existing text section to answer a question. However, it may not answer the question properly. It is like a school exam – listen carefully, read carefully and make sure you answer the actual questions!
Failing to understand what the client needs	Listening is essential. Do not second guess the client. If you are not entirely sure or want to check your understanding, ask.
Spending too much time telling the client how wonderful you are as a firm	They do need to know about your credentials and experience, but keep it to the point. However, they say they will see how good you are from the way you discuss their problems. They do not want to hear that your firm was established in 1892.
Using too many models, too much content, too many slides	Clients want a focused pitch that tells them exactly what they want to know. Fit your pitch into the time allowed.
Coming across as desperate	You are there because you have expertise. You are equal. They need you. Don't get hung up about the competition. Be proud of who you are and what you do. "A pitch meeting is like a date. You can smell if they're desperate and it's off-putting."
Not being relevant to the client	Make sure you are responding to their needs and not just saying what you want to say. What's in it for the client? Check every statement you make against this mantra.
Not following the rules set out for the pitch	Clients want to see you can stick to instructions so they know that they can work with you. If you have a specific length of time to present or are given a deadline, stick to it!
Not listening. Not allowing the client to comment enough. Not answering questions	Involving the client in the discussion allows you to build rapport and subtly change direction or messaging if you need to in order to respond to specific needs that arise.
Not understanding the client's motivations	Not understanding the business background of the client and then failing to translate this into an understanding of their motivations will deeply affect your chances of winning work.

continued on next page

Common mistakes	How to avoid them
Not researching the business or people enough	Researching a business does not mean just having a quick look at the website. It means understanding the long-term objectives, the sector, current trends and market threats, as well as its competitors. Understanding people's backgrounds helps you to make relationship connections and understand motives.
Leaving it to the last minute and rushing	Does this mean you are simply cutting and pasting and not tailoring to the client? Do you have enough time to understand your client's problem or business properly? It will be unlikely that you can produce a quality document or presentation and the danger is that embarrassing errors will creep in. It also puts unnecessary pressure on your team. People get frustrated, stressed and worried. Is this the way you want to present yourself to your client? Does it do your work justice?
Not knowing what is in your own pitch/proposal document	This is a common problem and is usually spotted quickly by the client. Some businesses feel that on occasion, they have known a law firm's proposal better than the firm did.
Not having a proper system in place for working on pitches	Do you have clear frameworks, resources and team roles for working on pitches? If you do, the production of a pitch or a presentation for a client will be efficient. It takes far less time to bring everything together.
Not presenting a cohesive or consistent message	It is important that the whole team is clear about the key messages and offerings to the target client and that everyone knows what has been said in the proposal paperwork. Everyone should be singing from the same hymn sheet.
Producing something that makes no sense to anyone other than yourself	It is always a good idea to ask someone else, outside of your work area, to read your pitch or proposal document or listen to your presentation. Often, when we write or speak, we assume knowledge in others that they do not have. We know exactly what we mean ourselves. By involving someone else, you can test your content and ensure that it is comprehensible.
Not making it interesting	The client on the receiving end of a pitch, particularly in the case of a tender or RFP response, will be reading the same information over and over again from different law firms. If you can make your responses interesting (eg, by employing some of the techniques described in this report), your material is more likely to stand out from the crowd.

continued on next page

Table 2. Common mistakes *Continued*

Common mistakes	How to avoid them
Poor writing and poor presentation	Businesses complain that the quality of the writing in legal proposals is poor. This is usually because it is too technical for a business audience or the writing style itself is not particularly readable. Good writing is a professional skill in itself and is not easy. Another issue is that the presentation is not designed well, which can inhibit the ease of reading. Too much text in too dense a layout is a common problem.
Not asking for feedback	It is a good idea to ask for feedback whether you win or lose a pitch. Constant self-appraisal of both your good and less good qualities will help you to continually develop and improve in terms of your client delivery. The simple process of asking for feedback also allows engagement with the target client. It may impress them and will help to establish a better relationship outside the confines of the pitch. You never know, you may get asked to do further work at a later date.

6. Receiving poor requests for proposals from business

> "We received an RFP from a renowned international brand. The document was so badly put together that it took two days to reorganise the information so that we could begin to make sense of it and start to understand what they were looking for."

It is more common than you would think for businesses to produce very poor RPF documents or specifications for the work they require. Lawyers will sometimes try to battle on and make sense of it themselves; however, this should be seen as an opportunity to contact the client and ask positive and interested questions. Any chance to make contact with a client during a formal or informal pitching situation should be seized in order to establish a closer relationship and a better understanding of their motivations and needs. It is worth noting that occasionally, during more formal pitching processes, contact with the client is not permitted during the tender submission phase.

> "One managing director said that a law firm turned up with 145 presentation slides. They had been very clear in their instructions that the initial pitch meeting would last only 30 minutes. The presentation was a disaster for everyone. He suspected the firm had simply dug out the standard presentation."

7. Pitching as the incumbent law firm

Pitching as the incumbent law firm is a hard position to be in. Businesses complain that firms only shake up their ideas just before a pitch. The law firm has had some years to keep abreast of the client's strategic and organisational changes, as well as changing market challenges. Many law firms fall into stagnant, transactional-based relationships without engaging with a client's business context on an ongoing basis. This can lead to dissatisfaction for the client and cause them to investigate other law firms in the market. The key to solving this is to remember that whenever you interact with a potential or existing customer, or even simply a contact, you must continually investigate their needs. Asking questions should become a habit.

**Can you answer these questions about your own clients?
Are you happy with your responses?**

1. Have you been working with the client for some time?

2. Have you kept abreast of their organisational changes and strategic needs?

3. Have you given them new ideas as you have gone along?

4. Where have you added real value?

5. How have you benefited them?

6. Have you delivered on your original promises?

7. Are you delivering at the same level as your competition?

8. Have you maintained the relationship well?

9. Do you have regular meetings – not to maintain the contract, but to discuss the business context for the client?

10. Do you do ongoing research about the client's market?

A good way to use these questions is to conduct an informal, internal review with your team on each client. If you are not happy with your answers to these questions, then you have time to do something about it and can improve the quality of your service.

"By understanding what the competition is offering, we can start to differentiate our own position in the marketplace and explain to our clients why they should use us and not someone else."

III. The context

1. Know the competition

Subconscious fear of intimidation can stop us looking at what the competition is doing. However, by understanding what the competition is offering, we can start to differentiate our own position in the marketplace and explain to our clients why they should use us and not someone else. By talking to business people and asking them why they use the lawyers they do, we can gain valuable information that will help us to refine our own selling arguments. By Googling our competition, we can find out how they are presenting themselves to their own clients. The amount of information they release about themselves online is phenomenal, and firms' own websites will describe in detail the services that they offer and their market positioning.

In order to pitch, you need to have a rough idea of what the competition will be saying. But don't get hung up about the competition. In public, they will always try to present their best side, just as you do; but they have faults and problems like anyone else.

You need to perceive the problems with your own firm from the client's point of view and tackle these while you are pitching. This way, you will have already dealt with their concerns and questions before they are allowed to fester or grow in the mind of the client.

> A very small niche firm was pitching against much larger law firms. They could envisage the concerns that the potential client would have over their ability to deliver the work. In the proposal document, they attacked this issue head on by explaining that, in reality, their highly specialist team of five was exactly the same size as the departmental team at a much larger firm. Therefore, they would be delivering the same amount of manpower; but because they were small, their service for that client would be far better.

It is important when you are pitching to a client that you do not openly criticise the competition. There are several reasons for this. First, it can make you look as though you feel somewhat inadequate in relation to them. Second, you never know whether you may need to work with them in the future. Lawyers move from firm to firm all the time and have friends or life partners at different firms. It is a small world. Being critical can create a bad impression of you or affect an attitude towards you. Being positive about your competition and yourself makes you appear confident, in control and assured about the strength of your position in the marketplace, your services, your skills and your ability to deliver what the client requires. Positivity and a self-assured attitude are attractive qualities to any client.

2. Know yourself

It is important that you are honest about your firm and its capabilities, both with yourself and with your target client, when you are making decisions about what you can and cannot do in terms of client work. When you are presenting to the client or sending in your proposal, you should highlight any areas where you will have to bring in extra support to enhance your capacity. This way, the client gets no surprises and knows they can rely on you to be straightforward and upfront.

Be prepared for questions about your moral and ethical stance on areas such as the environment and diversity, as well as your due diligence on suppliers and those you have commercial relationships and partnerships with. Do you have policies on these areas? Do you know where you and your firm stand on them?

> One very small firm recently was asked, when putting a proposal together, to provide their policy on modern slavery in terms of both themselves and their commercial partners. This came as a surprise, as they had never had to consider it before. However, in their client's industry, it was an area of serious concern. They have now put together a whole range of policies on various ethical and moral areas, so they are clear in their own minds and can talk to clients about their stance as a matter

> of course. These clear policies have given them a strong unique selling proposition (USP) for their size.

Establishing matching moral, ethical and business values with clients is becoming crucial in the current marketplace. Companies are concerned that they are consistent on this front within their entire business context. If you know that your firm is not strong in a particular area, do not pretend that it is. You can easily be caught out. Instead, maybe it is time for your firm to review its policies and behaviours to ensure that it has a modern standing in the marketplace – not only in terms of attracting new business, but also in terms of attracting and keeping top human capital.

> "The worst pitch I have ever seen was where the law firm totally misread us. Although I was in charge overall, the pitch was about an area that fell within the responsibilities of a female attorney. I was just there for the ride. It was her call. The lead attorney from the law firm turned his back to her and only addressed me throughout the meeting. He didn't even answer her questions. This reflected so badly on the firm. We could see they made poor decisions; they did not support diversity; they did not have empathy or listening skills. We could not work with the team."

"Being positive about your competition and yourself makes you appear confident, in control and assured about the strength of your position in the marketplace, your services, your skills and your ability to deliver what the client requires."

3. Relationship building

The pitching process and building relationships with target clients are long-term investments. While you are slowly building a relationship, you are constantly pitching your values, your skills and your relevance.

> The practice manager at one niche firm had a lot of experience of international pitching. He said that you have to be prepared to play the long game. For example, they had been doing speculative pitching and making approaches to firms in Japan for some 15 years. It had taken that amount of time and investment, and consistent work, to build up relationships, which were now starting to pay off. Even though it seemed a very long time, they were now ahead of the game. He could not emphasise enough the importance of getting to know people, understanding who they were and spending the time investing in the relationships.

Often, people walk away if they don't immediately get work; yet spending time fostering relationships pays real dividends in the long run. Maintaining contact means that you are at the forefront of the target client's mind if a piece of work comes up. If they send out an RFP, you'll be included on the list. You may already be the favoured firm simply because of the relationship you've invested in over time.

> One multimillion-pound property company was putting their audit out to tender. One of their non-exec directors said that she had had trouble having her preferred firm included on the list of those invited to respond to the tender. She said that the finance director had very clear preferences because of the relationships he had built up over several years, so he felt obliged to support that particular firm.

- Even if you don't win work the first time, build on the relationship, as there may be future opportunities.
- Keep giving to the contact and do not ask for anything. For example, you can make introductions for your target client to other contacts, send relevant information, meet the target client for coffees and give ideas and suggestions. The target client will feel an obligation to take reciprocal action. You do not need to ask for work.
- Ask if you can place staff on secondment at their business. Yes, there is a risk you may lose that staff member, but then you have a loyal and committed friend within the business who will carry your reputation further afield. They will always be grateful for having been given the opportunity and will give you opportunities in return. Most importantly, they will help you

understand that target client better and will influence positively within the target client's community.

- Be patient, because if they are continuing to engage with you, they are genuinely interested in you. It just may not be the right time at the moment for them.
- People work with people they like. If they know you, know what you do and that you are easy to access quickly, they will use you. They may refer you too.
- Continue to view clients as targets during your working relationship. Put as much work into maintaining the relationship as into building a new one. It is far easier to get more work from an existing relationship.

"Play the long game. Listen to us and be curious and interested. Take the time to hear what we say. Understand our challenges and problems. There will be a long-term return. You will get something if you stay in touch and add value in small ways. Remain relevant on the sidelines. Keep giving and never take. People will eventually give back."

4. Contextual advantages

There are other contextual activities that you can engage in, on a personal or business basis, which will help when trying to win new work. They provide a positive context and build your reputation in the marketplace. They can:

- build credibility;
- help you become more well known;
- build your professional reputation;
- demonstrate your technical excellence; and
- open the door to approaches for tenders and new business.

4.1. Profile building

Spending time developing and enhancing your personal, professional profile can be advantageous when it comes to business development and pitching. Many senior executives in business already invest in this area and lawyers and other professionals are beginning to do the same. LinkedIn has opened up opportunities to connect widely and make contact with other professionals in a way that we could not do before. Developing yourself as a speaker is another way to earn recognition and publicly demonstrate your expertise. This is impressive to any potential client. Many of us turn down opportunities to take on committee roles because of time commitments; however, these demonstrate seniority within the profession or within an industry.

The profession continually advocates thought leadership, which usually manifests itself in a firm's internal requirement for lengthy articles that are read by few people. Thought leadership can be demonstrated succinctly. A few lines on a simple LinkedIn post can be far more effective than a lengthy article in terms of getting a message across. Speaking opportunities, committee positions and associating with senior business people in photographs all demonstrate thought leadership through action. As said before, people buy people, and the more you are in the marketplace actively demonstrating your expertise, the more likely you are to be bought.

> One senior partner lives on a smallholding in New Zealand with her children. She raises sheep and other animals and makes preserves from the fruit they grow. She is writing a weekly diary on the challenges of running a firm and managing this smallholding. The juxtaposition of the two and their contrasting demands provides entertainment and humour. She has learned lessons from both and they help her to think differently about her work and her environment. This diary is now being sold to the press. It makes her a real person and it makes her interesting. It demonstrates her thought leadership and her values. Most importantly, it raises her profile.

4.2. Living your business values

> "Demonstrations of diversity are important in a proposal. We look at activities such as charitable endeavours. We want your values to match our business values."

Good businesses lead the way in terms of social and environmental values. Many now have environmental committees comprised of staff members and employees who are given time to engage in charitable and social responsibility activities. They are contributing to their communities. They actively believe in diversity, enhancing the rights of women and ethnic minorities, as well as the disabled, thereby recognising the richness and value that diversity brings to the culture and subsequent growth of a business.

The consumer marketplace has also changed in its ability to assess business activity and responsibility through social media. Social accountability has become paramount. Businesses proactively look to work with partners that support and share their values and will positively enhance their reputation.

> "We were impressed by one firm that came to meet us with three partners and a junior, female, foreign associate. We asked a question and one of the partners referred it to the junior staff member, as she would be working on the account. This told us a

lot about their firm, about the way they treated people, the trust they had in their staff and their ability to build a team."

Professional services firms must match these values with social responsibility programmes of their own so that they can work at an equal level with business. This does not mean paying lip service to it. It means living the values. It is transparent to any business if your behaviours do not reflect your stated values. If your firm is not keeping abreast of modern cultural and social developments, it is also likely to fall behind in its ability to win work.

If you can demonstrate your own social responsibility programmes and innovation, walk the talk and match business in the way they operate, you will have a strong platform from which to pitch. To show you understand business, you have to be a business, and that means behaving in the same ways.

IV. Approaching a pitch

1. Do we want to pitch?

It is completely normal to be enthusiastic and hopeful when you are asked to pitch for business. It means that you have done something right and it presents you with a doorway to new and exciting opportunities.

However, there are lots of reasons why businesses ask you to pitch. Sometimes, it is because they want someone else to compare their current supplier with. Occasionally, they will ask you simply to have another name on the list. They need a good number of potential firms to consider, but they do not think of you as a serious contender. For the most part, though, they will be genuinely interested in what you have to offer.

Judging where you sit with the client in terms of the pitch can be hard to gauge. The more realistic you are right from the start, particularly if you can communicate with the target client and assess the situation, the more likely you are to make a good decision as to whether you should pitch. If you are constantly pitching for work where you have no chance of winning – perhaps because you are not being considered as one of the key contenders or because you do not have quite the right experience – you are wasting time, money and energy. It can be demoralising for your team and for you if you keep losing, and this can affect your confidence in pitches where you do stand a good chance.

> "If you're pitching together, it's important that you are comfortable in each other's presence. If the group is nervous, it is off-putting for us. It tells us that you are out of your comfort zone. You are a professional and an expert. You should be showing off in your answers and feeling confident."

Stop and assess whether the pitch is good for you. It is easy to fall into a subservient mindset when pitching, running around after the client; but it is important to maintain your own confidence and with that the belief that you have the right to choose whether to pitch. You are an equal. They have asked you to pitch because they need your expertise. On recent pitching training seminars, this was the point that many found the most helpful. It changed their attitude fundamentally.

It is a good idea to keep a log of the time that you spend on pitches so that you get a view of their real cost. This will help you to decide either to invest more because it would be more economic to employ external help or to be more ruthless in cutting out those pitches that are too expensive to run for too little gain.

Table 3. Evaluating whether to pitch

Do we want to pitch?	Further evaluation questions
Is it good for our profile?	Is this work that will expose us to important decision makers? Is it high-profile work? Will it stretch us technically? Will it allow us to work above our usual level?
Is it something we want to do? Will it make us feel good?	Is this community project work? Is it a good morale builder for the team? Is it good for our portfolio? Is it just an amazing opportunity?
Is it financially sensible?	Does this project fit with our business plan? Is it financially sensible for us to take this on? Will we spend more time on this than we will be able to bill?
Is this the start of a future long-term relationship?	Do we believe in the client, the people and the business? Do we think this is a client that has a future and is going somewhere? If we take on a small amount of less profitable work now, will it lead to better opportunities in the future? Do we know anything about the working relationship with their current law firm?

continued on next page

Do we want to pitch?	Further evaluation questions
Is there a good fit between their business and our firm?	Do we have lots of experience with similar businesses? Is this within our core skills and experience? Do we have similar business values? Do they work in a similar way?
Is the process organised?	Are they chaotic in the way they have organised the pitch process? Does this reflect how they are likely to do business?
Do we need to make investments to take on the work?	Can we do the work now or will we need to invest in new resources? Is this going to be wise in the longer term?
Are there international or cultural differences?	Do our business cultures fit? If we are very different, will it cause conflict on the job? Will we be able to accommodate these factors? Will we be able to access relevant expertise if necessary?
Could we deliver the work if we won?	Do we have the skills? Do we have the resources? Do we have the time? Do we have the capacity?
Is it an industry we want to be in?	Is this an industry we already have experience in? Is this an industry we want to gain experience in? Is this an exciting new market?
Will there be the right financial reward?	Do they have a big enough budget to pay for the work? Are they looking for someone cheap?
Are we being asked to pitch to fill the list?	Do we still have a chance of winning? Will we create a good relationship and open doors for the future even if we don't win? Is it a complete waste of time?
Is the client on a fishing trip?	Are they looking to gain advice and information without paying? What is their track record?
Do they fit with our values?	Are they ethical? Do we respect them and the way they do business? Do we want to be associated with them?
Do they treat us with respect?	Will they listen to advice? Will there be a blame culture?
Have we background checked the client?	Investigate the company. Are they financially stable? How much can be found out about them? Do they have reputational issues? Is the client still suitable?

continued on next page

Table 3. Evaluating whether to pitch *Continued*

Do we want to pitch?	Further evaluation questions
Do we have a good relationship with the personnel?	Do we have good relationships with the business? Will the pitch be run by procurement, in which case relationships are less important? Do we know that the person heading up the pitch has a close relationship with another firm? Have we lost pitches with this person before? Will it come down to the relationship at the end of the process?

Once you have actively made the decision to pitch, you can move on to the research process.

2. Do the preparation and research

Good preparation and research are the foundations of a good result. Do not underestimate the advantages that you can give yourself by going the extra mile with your research.

> "We were pitching to an international client. After in-depth research online, we found the entire speech the chief executive had given earlier that year at the staff annual conference. It outlined all the strategic aims and objectives that the staff had to deliver against over the coming year. They would be measured against these in their performance appraisals. We were able to use these aims and objectives to structure our entire pitch. We demonstrated how we could support them in what they were trying to achieve, help them meet their performance targets internally and genuinely add value through the work we were doing for them. They were extraordinarily impressed with our presentation and the depth of our understanding. We won the client."

Researching in-depth can give you an advantage over the competition. Many lawyers have a quick look at the website. This is not enough. With so much information available online, it is possible to find out a great deal about your client and the challenges they are facing. In fact, anything or everything that you can find will help you to put together a better picture of your client and their business performance. It will build your understanding and knowledge of the market that they are operating within. This will bear fruit, as it demonstrates to the client the level of your business acumen and attention to detail. This will set you apart from the competition; or at least, will not let the competition have an advantage over you.

For example, you can investigate:

- press coverage and media releases;
- company annual reports;
- profiles of individual directors on LinkedIn;
- strategic documents;
- articles written by the personnel involved;
- marketplace reports;
- their performance in the marketplace;
- their customers and their products;
- materials they have produced for their own clients; and
- YouTube videos.

Collating all the research information so that everybody on your team has access to it and can get a good overview is useful. There are two good ways to do this, which can be used in conjunction with one another. Platforms such as Google Drive, or an internal equivalent, allow you to keep all your information together practically. It can also be an excellent motivator, and help others with different learning styles, to display the information about the client around the office. This immersion in the pitch can help to generate imaginative ideas, better insights and a sense of ownership. It will also drive the desire to win within the entire team, which will result in better work.

> "Always do thorough research. Even if you don't win the business this time, you want to impress us enough to be in the picture next time. Otherwise, you are just killing future income streams."

3. Who are our targets?

Working out who you are pitching to is essential for the success of any meeting, presentation or proposal document. It will completely change the tone, the style, the emphasis and the format of the information you present. For example, if you are writing material for a business CEO, you will be writing in a completely different style compared to how you would write for in-house counsel. If you are preparing a proposal document or a presentation/meeting for both of these people within the same business, you could present an executive summary of the key business issues and benefits for the CEO, followed by a separate section on all the legal technical issues and credentials required by the lawyer. This way, you satisfy the information needs of both.

Although people will claim publicly that the decisions they make are based on rational analysis, the reality is that there are usually emotional drivers to their decisions. People like to work with people that they trust and can relate to. For some people, that trust is built through technical excellence. For others, it comes from the ability to have a friendly relationship with the person they are working with. Sometimes, it is because they feel a particular firm's work will make them look good internally. Do not underestimate the emotional input in a purchasing decision. Working out the emotional drivers for each individual is vital.

Nobel prize winner Daniel Kahneman explored decision making and looked at two systems for making decisions. System 1, which is based on fast, instinctive and emotional factors, is generally thought to account for 90% of all decision making. System 2, which is based on deliberate logic, is thought to account for only 10% of decisions made. Working out the distinctive emotional factors in our target clients is truly important for the pitching process. However, your targets are likely to rationalise their own decisions to themselves and their colleagues through evidence and logical argument. Their own emotional drivers may well be subconscious. It is essential, therefore, to feed both needs for our target clients.

Usually, more than one person is involved in the decision to purchase services. We need to identify who these people are and the level of influence that they have over the decision. You can do this by asking direct questions, listening to the subtext of conversations, looking for information about the business and personnel online, as well as using your own networks and business contacts as sources. The influencers are not always obvious.

"In-house counsel are now under a lot of pressure to use procurement departments to buy legal services and there is a lot of discussion about this. Many in-house lawyers are trying to resist this change because they fear that procurement teams do not understand the area or they believe that these teams will affect the relationships with their current suppliers; and sometimes they do not like the interference."

"One more formal pitch we did had a very complex set of influencers and decision makers. We knew that the owners of the business were entrepreneurs. But we knew we would also be dealing with internal technical staff of different disciplines. Then we had to go through an external consultancy company that was filtering the proposal documents to make a shortlist. We wanted to learn more about the entrepreneurs and so watched clips of them on YouTube. In every clip, they mentioned their chairman and we realised that he would be a key influencer in the decision, although he wasn't mentioned as part of the pitch panel at any point. We were able to learn details about their business objectives, get personality pointers and find out about their interests and motivators from the YouTube clips. For example, the business had been started by their father, so maintaining a sense of family belonging with all their staff had remained key during their development and growth. We were able to put together a proposal that not only appealed to their sense of family, but also presented information suitable for, and tailored to, the different personalities we had to appeal to."

4. Dealing with the procurement department

Many lawyers believe that if you are dealing with procurement departments, you may as well produce your standard proposal document and the cut-and-paste approach is as good as any. It is an area that lawyers seem nervous of and are unsure about how best to deal with. Procurement is often raised by lawyers as a point of concern. However, the procurement department still consists of people. They will be able to tell how well you have researched their business. They will be looking for certain types of information within the document that helps them to meet their own objectives and requirements. Don't forget, you can ask questions of procurement too.

In-house counsel are now under a lot of pressure to use procurement departments to buy legal services and there is a lot of discussion about this. Many in-house lawyers are trying to resist this change because they fear that procurement teams do not understand the area or they believe that these teams will affect the relationships with their current suppliers; and sometimes they do not like the interference. However, they are fighting a losing battle, as there is growing momentum within business to move to this model. For many years, business has felt that legal expenses have been too high. This probably results from an aggressively competitive marketplace where legal firm partners have felt under pressure to reach overambitious targets and so have perhaps billed clients harder than they should have done or let billable hours run higher than the client expected.

Businesses are now hitting back and are looking for good value in what they know to be an overcrowded marketplace. Value does not necessarily mean cheap; but it does mean that clients want a better grip on the purchase of their external legal services so they can be sure of what they are getting. In fact, it has been said that engaging legal services in conjunction with the procurement department can reduce legal spend by 15% to 20% (a rough statistic). The idea is that the decisions of the procurement department are based on data and information, rather than on the subjective relationships of the in-house lawyer. Procurement within legal services is here to stay, so the only thing we can do is embrace it and work with it.

It is important to try to imagine the procurement end users as best you can. A procurement department is still made up of people and they also have drivers in terms of their own work and delivery. They will look to where legal suppliers can help them with these.

In order to understand how to appeal to the procurement department, it is important to grasp their role and purpose. From this, we can deduce what they will be looking for in terms of legal services, how they will be supporting their in-house lawyers, what the pressures on them are and how we can contribute.

Procurement is very different from purchasing and the two are regularly confused. Purchasing is the functional buying of items for a business. Procurement is a strategic business discipline that looks to get the best value it can for services, while working within business objectives and ensuring that contracts are well managed. The procurement team will need to answer not only to the in-house legal department, but also to other directors such as finance and the CEO. The personnel within the procurement department can often be lawyers themselves or have backgrounds in contract law.

The roles the procurement department plays within legal services are:

- researching the best firms in the marketplace. Sometimes that may involve looking for a large firm for a particular function; at other times, it may be that they need a sole practitioner with a specialist niche skill;
- looking for the best value (the best work at the best price to fill the need, not necessarily the cheapest);
- forecasting price trends;
- developing purchasing strategies;
- evaluating proposals on commercial and technical factors;
- ensuring that law firms are aware of their business objectives and work within them;
- establishing fees and payment terms;

"It is important to try to imagine the procurement end users as best you can. A procurement department is still made up of people and they also have drivers in terms of their own work and delivery. They will look to where legal suppliers can help them with these."

- strategically vetting law firms – for example, on ethical and reputational factors;
- negotiating contracts;
- ensuring quality work;
- reviewing the account formally;
- maintaining a good working relationship with the law firm;
- ensuring that performance targets are set and met;
- project managing the account successfully in order to increase efficiency, including looking to automation where possible;
- producing reports and statistics on spending; and
- evaluating the marketplace and predicting where further services and legal needs may arise.

"The law firm were pitching to me, but I had one eye on how I would use the information with my CEO, my CFO, my team and the procurement function."

You can therefore appeal to procurement by evaluating these roles and producing arguments that answer these points within your proposal. For example, you can help them by:

- producing information for other directors within the business (eg, CFO, CEO);

- producing material that is tailored to their business objectives and offering to write future reports in this way;
- stating the value to the business of each activity you would undertake;
- comparing the value you bring against others in the marketplace;
- providing ideas and methods for measurement that will allow them to report internally;
- presenting ways of managing the account which will make life easy for them;
- suggesting pricing models that are at the forefront of the market or promising to update continually in light of market changes, thereby ensuring good value for procurement;
- putting forward ways to help them measure the quality of your work;
- ensuring that your ethical and reputational factors fit with theirs and explaining these to them;
- offering to produce reports in the formats that they require (eg, spend versus value);
- being flexible in terms of the contract and pricing. Trying to get to grips with what they need to achieve, even by asking them direct questions, will show them that you listen and are

"Establishing the personality traits of your targets will help you in deciding on the tone, the emphasis, the structure and the content of any meeting, presentation or proposal document you produce."

prepared to adapt to work with them as a responsible partner; and
- predicting future needs. If you can help them to see and understand these needs, making them 'look good', they can then become your advocate within the business.

5. Panels

> "If you've got through the panel process to a meeting, then your information is fine and so is everyone else's. That's not how the decision will be made. We want to see what sort of relationship we're going to have with you."

Selection panels can be made up of different disciplines within the business, including in-house lawyers, procurement staff and external consultants. These panels will often use rating mechanisms, which vary depending on the RFP requirements. Each person on the panel rates the firm and sometimes different aspects on their selection criteria can carry more weight. They then look to see which firm has scored the most. Even at this stage, they can add a firm back in if they feel it was very good, but perhaps didn't score as highly as expected. This is why it is so important to work to impress them in as many ways as possible. Once you are through this stage, in-house lawyers say:

> "Yes, the end decision is probably emotional. There has to be chemistry with the firm and you have to feel that there is mutual respect."

6. Personality traits

Establishing the personality traits of your targets will help you in deciding on the tone, the emphasis, the structure and the content of any meeting, presentation or proposal document you produce. Different personalities require different types of information and need it presented in different ways. We often see this demonstrated in personal relationships at home. Where one person in the family may need information to be given as facts, another may need more context or more about the emotion and feelings behind the issue concerned. For example, someone may be upset about something and another person might begin to try to fix the problem and tell them where they could have done things differently, rather than listening and giving empathy. This leads to family arguments! If you try to give the wrong sort of information in the wrong format to an individual, they will feel dissatisfied, as they do not have what they need to fulfil their psychological requirements.

In a business context, there are many different models for defining personality types. To make it easier, these have been compressed

Table 4. Personality types

Personality groups and qualities of your target	Information type and style required from you
TYPE 1: ANALYTICAL – introvert, likes facts	
• Methodical • Often technically minded in their profession • Logical • Accurate • Consistent • Finds it hard to express opinions directly • Likes to work alone or in very small groups • Makes decisions based on data and evidence • Rational • Asks many questions • Can suffer from indecision through too much analysis	• Detailed • Accurate • Facts and figures • Technical • In-depth knowledge • Data and evidence • Steady, calm and rational • Targets and measurable goals • Think through pros and cons
TYPE 2: AMIABLE – introvert, likes people	
• Encouraging • Friendly • Relaxed and likes a peaceful environment • Feels empathy • Likes people • Team player • Often makes decisions with others • Good at bringing people together • Not controversial • Doesn't like upsetting people • Often waits until the last minute to make decisions and then goes with what everyone else is doing • Likes to be guided by others' expertise	• Easy-going, friendly introduction at a meeting • Build rapport • Give them strong direction on what to do • A mix of data, graphics and top-line information • Not too in-depth • Team approach • Recognition of everyone's contribution

into four simplistic groups in Table 4, based on the Merrill-Wilson breakdown – although interestingly, the ideas go back to ancient Greek times. We are all composed of traits of the four types of personality, but the leading personality trait will define how we prefer to receive information. Most of us can recognise people we know in each of these groups, although they may not have all the traits identified in the list.

Personality groups and qualities of your target	Information type and style required from you
TYPE 3: EXPRESSIVE – extrovert, likes people	
• Flamboyant • Can overcommit to please • Emotional • Performer • Energetic • Outgoing and friendly • People orientated • Eloquent communicator • Motivational/persuasive • Imaginative and creative • Generates new ideas • Can be very up or very down	• Pictures and graphics • Big-picture ideas and results • People focused • Entertaining communication • Well-communicated presentations, with humour if possible • Conversational interaction • Opportunity to involve them • Innovative, smart and new ideas
TYPE 4: DRIVER – extrovert, likes facts	
• Highly assertive • Results/action focused • Seem very dominant • Works alone • Makes decisions, often without consultation, and can be seen as ignoring the needs of others • Disciplined • Does not chat • Solves emotional problems through action • Speaks very directly, sometimes to the point of giving offence	• Only the information they require • Clear, measureable results • Get straight to the point • Do not waste time • Clear graphics and evidence, not detailed • Big-picture outline • Clear actions you are going to take

Using all the sources of information that we have, we can start to analyse the type of person our target is. For example, say we are going to meet with Jane, the managing director of a marketing agency. From LinkedIn, we can see that she enjoys creative writing and belongs to several relevant groups. The writing style that her profile is written in is goal oriented, puts forward top-line points and is concise. We can also see from searching on Google that the agency has won several business awards for results-driven activities. We learn from our contacts that Jane does colourful public speaking. From this information, we can make an educated guess that she is probably an 'expressive' personality type.

Following this assessment, we can begin to think about how we might present information to Jane. Jane is likely to want top-line information with support from graphics and picture images. She will probably want the meeting to be focused on the actions you intend to carry out for her business and the advantages these will bring. She will want to contribute and will prefer an interactive meeting where there is plenty of conversation, where she can contribute her thoughts and opinions, and where she feels listened to. She will enjoy a lively, if not funny, interaction with you.

This process is not scientific, but can help you to focus your own thoughts in preparation for meeting your target and encourage you to think about how you will structure your arguments and what areas to concentrate on.

Table 5 contains a list of questions which will help you to think about your targets, whether you are planning a meeting, a lunch or a formal pitch.

Table 5. Questions to consider when planning a pitch

Who will be present?	Is it a one-on-one meeting? Will it be a panel? Have you actually asked the questions or have you made assumptions? It is easy to get caught out.
Who is the decision maker? Who are the influencers?	You can ask questions in advance to try to establish this. Doing your research about the business and the people involved can help you to make an educated guess. However, do not be fooled into thinking that it is always somebody senior. On one pitch, it was the junior member staff who was in charge of that section. She was the decision maker and the senior people were influencers. Sometimes you can work out who is actually the key decision maker during a meeting if you are alert and aware of the interpersonal dynamics going on. If you provide information for everyone, which appeals to their individual needs and motivations, you will have covered all bases.
Have you researched each individual?	Using LinkedIn or Google to investigate individual backgrounds can give you valuable information in terms of their personalities and interests. For example, on LinkedIn, you can see the interest groups they have signed up to. In one meeting, it was noted that the target had expressed an interest in animal welfare and was signed up to various groups through LinkedIn. This changed the tone of the meeting, as he showed everyone his beautiful wild animal photography at the start.

continued on next page

What are their personal motivators, values and issues of concern?	These can be both business and personal. Both can impact on your result. One lawyer discovered on Google that his target had an ongoing court case at work where he had made a mistake. As a result, the client was sensitive to technical excellence and attention to detail. He needed to be reassured that there would be clarity in communication and technical care, and that the firm had credibility and experience in doing similar work. The pitching lawyer did not need to mention his awareness of the court case. He simply needed to structure his evidence, conversation and tone around the emotional needs of the target.
Are there any business context issues which will be affecting them personally?	Changes of personnel, recent promotions, poor financial results, restructuring and mergers: all these business aspects will affect the pressure and the environment that your target is experiencing at work, and will have an emotional and stress impact on them. Being aware of these will help you to address subtext issues and give you the opportunity to demonstrate your knowledge of their business and where they are going. You may be able to contribute or help in some way.
What sort of personality are they? How are they going to want information presented?	It is not an exact science, but a lot can be deduced simply from the writing style of their LinkedIn profile. If it is short and to the point, then that is probably how they like information presented to them. If they are technically specialist, they will probably want technical detail. If you are meeting an entrepreneur, they are likely to want an executive business summary with graphics, which is short and sweet. An accountant will want facts and detailed supporting figures with evidence-based arguments.
Can you use your personal or firm contact network to find out more about, for example, internal conflicts?	Any inside information will help with interpreting internal dynamics, conflicts, politics and other factors that may affect their decision about you. This sort of information may change your decision to pitch in the first place. In one case, personal contacts led to an invitation to an event where the chairman of the target business was speaking to a small audience about the company's future ambitions and strategies. The lawyers were able to sound highly knowledgeable and engaged in a meeting with the target client later that week, as well as being able to tailor their material accordingly.

7. Putting together your account team

The other advantage of analysing the target personalities is that you can put together a team that will work well when interacting with the prospect. For example, an artistic personality type may not respond as well to a meeting with analytical personality types. They may work better with people who have easy-going personality traits. Always assess what each team member will bring to that client in terms of value.

> "Why are the different people on your team present during a pitch meeting? What role does each of them play? When I was young we were pitching to a Swedish company. I was too junior to be of much help technically, but I did speak some Swedish. They took me along so that I could chat over drinks."

8. Unique selling proposition: why buy us?

Understanding where your firm stands out in the marketplace and being able to articulate what is special about it will provide you with a strong base for pitching your business as a whole. It will also contribute to the constant reinvention and rethinking that are necessary in order to stay ahead of the game. When you pitch, you need to think about what you can do better for the client than anyone else. Are you more specialised in a particular area? Can you provide evidence of this? Do you stand for certain values that may appeal to your client and present a different firm image compared to everyone else (eg, you are a paper-free business and take a stand on green issues)? Are you better value for money, although perhaps not necessarily cheaper? You need to understand the client, their motivations and their business well enough that you can use all relevant arguments in your armoury and know that they will appeal to them.

> One accountancy firm was preparing to submit a proposal for a government tender. It occurred to them that they received regular training in-house on the specialist areas that they were being invited to submit a proposal on to the government department. They realised that if they offered free training to the government officials who would be managing the project, it would give them a USP for a number of reasons:
>
> - It would help them to build a relationship with the government staff by getting to know them better on the training courses.
> - It would increase the government officials' knowledge of the area, allowing them to work more productively with the accountancy firm.

- Budget within government departments is always very tight and the offer of free technical training for staff as an enhancement to the scope of the project would be very attractive to them. It would cost the accountancy firm little, but would be of high value to the government staff concerned.

9. Brand context

Many people believe that their firm brand is enough of a USP in itself. The reality is that, within the professional services sector, there is very little in terms of real differentiation. All firms declare themselves to be committed to the client, to be technically excellent, to act as the client's partner and to have a business-like approach. However, clients are sophisticated, and these factors are expected as standard and 'the norm' when they buy legal services. Differentiation must be on top of these basics. Within the general business sector and within social media, there has been a tidal move towards 'tribalism' – in other words, large cross-societal groups that believe in or lobby for an issue, or that have a common identifying factor. Firms and businesses that can tap into these tribal groups can make a real impact.

For example, one highly successful real estate agency in Vancouver has set itself up as a pioneer for animal welfare.

"Many people believe that their firm brand is enough of a USP in itself. The reality is that, within the professional services sector, there is very little in terms of real differentiation. All firms declare themselves to be committed to the client, to be technically excellent, to act as the client's partner and to have a business-like approach."

> They have worked with cosmetics companies that do not experiment on animals; they raise money for welfare lobbying groups; they make political representations; and the CEO adopts chickens from battery farms. As a result, the CEO is regularly photographed and interviewed by the press. She speaks publicly and writes articles on the issue. It has gained the agency a lot of exposure and a strong, committed following. Either clients are impressed because the agency is well known or they choose to work with it because they believe in animal welfare too.

A small number of professional services firms are starting to define themselves by identifying with values or with a way of working, but these are currently few and far between.

> A small litigation firm in Brussels has concentrated on becoming a paper-free office. This has become an integral part of their brand and sets them apart from their competition. It has won them business.
>
> A specialist, small retail accountant in the Midlands in the United Kingdom has established itself as a purely online service. All meetings are done via Skype, all accounts are managed on online platforms and all communication is done via email. They work without paper and the staff and management are agile workers. They have none of the overheads of an office. Their clients appreciate the fact that they can manage their accounts at any time, which is a great help within the small retail sector, and the fact they have greater access and freedom to contact their accountant, because Skype is so much easier than a physical meeting. Pricing is also highly competitive because there are few overheads.

The bottom line is that you must be realistic about your own brand. Is it strong enough? Is it actually a USP in itself? Or do your brand and your USP need some work?

Do not make the mistake of letting your brand get out of proportion. Within professional services, your brand should be like a picture frame. A frame is there to show a picture at its best and should be complementary in style to the picture within. The people in your firm are the picture and the brand is there to complement you and provide a strong, cohesive frame for what you do. Too often, over the last 20 years, the brand has become more important than the people in the firm. The brand has become the picture and all the people in the firm cling to the outside in an attempt to have some relevance.

People buy people. That is why they ask for referrals to individual lawyers and not necessarily to firms. That is why they want to meet with you. It's about trust and relationships. The overpowering branding that has taken place within the professional services sector has forgotten the basics of professional services selling. The brand has become more important than the lawyer. The current move towards tribalism, combined with the strength of individual representation and opinion on social media, is advantageous. It will allow professionals to be real people again and celebrate who they are and what they offer their clients. It will kick the brand back to where it belongs.

When you are pitching, you need to be sure of your picture frame – your brand – and what it is and what it stands for. It is what binds your team together; but you can be different people within that. The potential client will choose you on the basis of their trust for you and their potential relationship with you, and your brand should support that by being complementary and providing a strong context.

10. Credentials

It is common to see credentials that list the work you have done and the firms you have worked for without highlighting the benefits that you have brought for the client. What was the advantage to the client? How did you add extra value? If you keep these questions at the forefront of your mind, even when working with your current clients, you will be able to provide a better ongoing service and to demonstrate how you are actively adding value, rather than falling into a transactional relationship with them.

Having a selection of well-written case studies in your portfolio can help you to demonstrate a whole range of experience and skills, as well as the 'added value' that you bring. Case studies are regularly poorly written and are not focused on the client's interests.

The following headings will help you to structure your case studies to ensure that they are focused in the right way:

- Who was the client and/or what industry are they in?
- Are they national or was there an international aspect?
- Were you working for in-house lawyers or for the board? How did you relate to and communicate with them to give them what they needed?
- What was the client's problem?
- How were you able to solve this for the client?
- What specialist skills or experience did you have for this particular work? Why were you the right choice for the client? How did you make their life easy?

- How did you benefit the client? Were are you able to bring extra value?
- What was the end result? Was the client's problem solved?
- Are you able to ask for a testimonial or a quote from the client?

By focusing the case studies on the client's problems, rather than on your abilities, you are demonstrating your client-centric thinking and talking about issues that other potential clients can easily relate to.

"I visited the office of an in-house lawyer. I had recently produced a proposal and I asked her what she thought of it and whether it was alright. She said, 'I have absolutely no idea. I don't know which is yours. I can't tell one from the other, they are all so similar.' She then pointed to a pile of about 20 identical-looking documents on a table in the corner. This opened my eyes to how difficult it was to stand out and that was a real lesson for me."

11. The client's specifications: reading between the lines

If you are fortunate enough to receive a specification document, an outline or an RFP from the client concerning their needs, this can give you a number of clues as to the context and the issues that are actually affecting the client. This is about us defining their real needs as opposed to taking what they state in their document at face value.

"Do not be afraid of asking questions. Your target client may well be impressed with your perceptiveness."

"When we were reading a New Zealand government RFP, they actually stated within the text that they needed to increase their own knowledge of the particular technical area in question. We were able to translate this fact into an approach for the pitch. We did not go into great technical detail. Instead, we used our credentials to demonstrate our expertise in this area and to build trust. We made the text easy to understand and offered to work with them, including running specialist seminars, in order to help increase their knowledge of the area. We were encouraging and positive without being patronising in order to build their confidence in us, so that they would feel that we would support them. They had also listed the criteria by which submissions would be evaluated. For each question, we carefully gave them the information they required. Then, as the final part of the question, we summarised the key points we were making under subheadings which were in fact their own evaluation criteria. By doing this, we made the job of evaluating our submission very easy for them: it ensured that we were meeting and exceeding every criterion on each and every question. We won this contract."

Careful interpretation of the text allows you to register deeper meanings, needs and motivations behind the search for a new firm. The language itself can give clues.

"The text stated that they wanted a relationship with the law firm that was respectful. They said that they were keen to listen to their advisers and were good at acting on guidance. It seemed a strange statement until we looked further into the background of this successful, family-run business. It transpired that the business had been founded by the father and that he had had a reputation for not taking advice. In the end, he had fallen out with his own board and they had parted on bad terms. The board and his son, who was now running the business, were very sensitive about this. We translated this knowledge into statements concerning partnership, respect, equality in the relationship and the importance of good communication. We reflected back to them the behaviours that they keenly wanted to see."

If you make an interpretation of their language or text, but are not entirely sure of its validity, there is the opportunity to ask questions in a careful way that will allow you to explore your understandings and establish whether they have legs. Do not be afraid of asking questions. Your target client may well be impressed with your perceptiveness. You can also use your background research to look for evidence to support your conclusions.

"They talked extensively about their 'family' of staff, but were looking to expand globally. The text was littered with terminology such as 'next step', 'moving forward' and 'new opportunities'. We knew they already had a law firm, but quickly realised that this firm was unable to deliver the global overview that they now required and that we could provide through our international legal network. The regular use of the terminology told us that this was a brave step for them, and that they were probably quite nervous. They had built their business on staff who had been loyal to them for a long time and who were comfortable in their familiar Australian environment. We were able to give them reassurance about our ability to support them, and that when dealing with overseas contacts and issues, we would be able to establish friendly and helpful relationships that they could depend on. We took the fear away for them, made it easy and inspired the staff with the potential of the opportunities they had in front of them."

12. Theme and style

On completion of the research stage, a decision can be made about the theme and the style of your approach to the target client. The theme will encompass:

- the key messages that you wish to convey to the client;
- the key issues for the client; and
- the client's motivators.

The style you decide upon will incorporate:

- the tone you will adopt;
- the appearance of any materials;
- design factors; and
- a 'personality' you might give to a presentation (eg, lively, factual).

Your theme and style should be written into a short statement for you or your team. This will allow the team to be consistent in the work that they do and ensure that they are all singing from the same hymn sheet.

If it is just for you, writing yourself some notes to add to the file will help you to pick up relationships quickly in the future and to prepare for any one-to-one meetings.

Overall, this ensures integration of all parts of your pitch, no matter what or who was the source, presenting one clear voice to the client.

Below is an example of what a theme statement and style outline might look like.

Extension of your staff family

They are extremely relationship driven. We can see that they look to partner with people who complement their own skills and plug their weaknesses, which we feel reflects the need for a partnership approach.

We have the expertise and unique technical capabilities to support them. For us, it's about being partners – upping the game; asking the hard questions; challenging them. If they want someone that's going to be there, fully invested in their business, an extension to their team, someone that thinks outside the box and will ask the hard questions, stretch them, bring the best thinking from our own global community – and in doing so, extend their global community – that's us!

They live and breathe their brand visually through their colours. We can reflect this throughout the documentation and integrate their design themes and colours with our own in order to represent the fact that we are an extension of their staff family and part of their team. Written and oral communications should reflect their own communications and their brand values – colourful, positive, youthful, energetic and challenging. They use short words, which are often modern or slightly slang, and they make jokes. We will use similar language and humour.

13. Pricing

Pricing is a very sensitive area, but it is an area where business thinks quite differently from law firms. Business is used to thinking in terms of cost and value. When businesses spend money, they want to see demonstrable return on their investment (ROI). Many businesses comment on specific issues they see with law firms in this area.

They want to see that:

- you are sensitive to cost;
- you are cost effective;
- you understand the business of law and can understand their finances (eg, read a balance sheet, grasp their operating income);
- you can speak their language and demonstrate how you will bring ROI;
- you are pricing using the latest models and frameworks; and
- you are competitive in the marketplace.

They do not want you just to state the problem they have and the cost of fixing it. They want to understand the value you are going to bring to their business.

14. Drawing the relevant material and points together

Once you know who you are presenting to or meeting with, and have done a rough personality analysis, you can start thinking about the overall balance between facts and evidence, credential information and emotional motivators in the arguments that you present to them.

> "We found ourselves meeting with the accountant, the information technology and technical developments directors and an MD with an artistic personality type. We decided to split the information into three, providing each with their own version of the pitch. They all received an executive summary. The accountant received a set of figures and information relevant to his needs. The technical and information technology directors received evidence and facts, and the MD received a briefing highlighted with graphics and top-line information. It outlined the benefits of the work we would be doing and the positive impact on the people within the organisation and customers. He was also presented with a communications framework and we emphasised how important two-way communication was within the client relationship. We gave the MD plenty of opportunity to give his opinion."

The common mistake is to include far too much information. Editing heavily at this point will save a great deal of time later in terms of writing and editing a written document or in thinking how to structure a meeting or a presentation. Returning to the mantra "What's in it for the client?" will make the decision about what to keep and what to reject far easier.

> "I was putting together a proposal document and the partner sent me 256 pages of general information that he wanted to include. Most of it was not relevant."

Keep it succinct. Be very honest with yourself. What persuades and what is boring and irrelevant? It is far better to have clear space in your document or clear airtime in a meeting than to have it crammed with too much material. You will be able to put across short, relevant messages that the client will be far more likely to take on board because they are not hidden in a stream of innocuous points. The likelihood is that your competition will be delivering a stream of information about themselves rather than points honed to your client's needs and motivations. You will stand out.

"Once you know who you are presenting to or meeting with, and have done a rough personality analysis, you can start thinking about the overall balance between facts and evidence, credential information and emotional motivators in the arguments that you present to them."

> "If you buy a drill, it's not because you want drill; it's because you want a hole in the wall. People buy law firms because they want them to solve a problem. It's important that the law firm understands the business and what it wants."

If you are writing a response to an RFP, do not fall into the trap of using your key messages as the starting point for your answers to their questions. The danger here is that you stop reading the question and simply say what you want to say. The client has chosen to include specific questions because they require factual information and need to find out more about you in order to compare you to other firms. It is rather like exams. You must read the question carefully and make sure you answer it. Yes, you want to include your key messages in order to influence and persuade; but build these into the answers, not the other way round. The client also needs to see that you can follow instructions. If you cannot answer specific questions when they are written out, it does not bode well for the client work that you will produce. Give them the information they need. Frequently, businesses complain that lawyers do not answer the questions asked of them precisely, but simply cut and paste what they want to say into the box.

> A member of the UK government's insolvency service raised this issue. He said that lawyers regularly do not read the

specifications and so do not tailor the answers properly or respond to questions appropriately.

15. Good writing

The author Nathanial Hawthorne once wrote, "Easy reading is damn hard writing." How very right he was. There are very good writers in the legal profession, but it is a common complaint from business that much of what they are sent is difficult to understand.

These are the common problems:

- It is too wordy.
- It does not necessarily get across the points clearly.
- It assumes too much knowledge of the reader.
- It uses technical language or abbreviations without explanation.
- It is written for the writer, not the reader.
- It lacks relevance for the reader and does not engage the reader's interest.
- It is too technical.

The more technical the subject is, the clearer the writing needs to be.

During one regular business meeting, a paper outlining a new legal issue was due for consideration. The management team had all received the paper in advance. The chairman asked whether anyone wanted to kick off the discussion and there was silence. Finally, the newest member of team spoke up and said they had read the paper, but had failed to understand what on earth it was about. Everyone laughed and then they all confessed that none of them had understood the paper. The writer of the paper had not managed to convey any information or points to his readers. He had shut down their interest entirely. If this had been a pitch situation, the law firm would have lost at first base. The lawyer in this case was lucky. He was asked to rewrite the paper so they could all understand it.

If you have a good writer on your team or are a good writer yourself, that is a benefit. If you are dubious about the writing skills that you have access to, then it may be advisable to hire someone to take on this work for you. Firms are reluctant in many instances to hire this sort of support. However, it makes little sense to take an expensive fee earner away from income-generating client work in order to do a poor writing job, rather than letting someone who is highly skilled at writing do the work for you at what is likely to be a fraction of the cost of the fee earner.

A skilled writer will not only be able to ensure that you have answered the questions properly, but will craft paragraphs that include your key messages and points in a persuasive, cohesive and eloquent way. They will be economic with words and tailor the text to the client, if they are well briefed. They will also be able to adopt any style or tone you wish to present.

Asking someone else in a different department or a friend in business to read the final text is a good idea. Someone else reading the material cold will pick up on points that do not make sense or could be better explained. This is particularly important when pitching to business people rather than other lawyers. This will also ensure that the focus in the document is correct and emphasises the client's interest. Some larger firms have a specific team whose job it is to go through proposal documents and presentations as though they are the client in order to highlight problems and produce a better-quality result.

> One medium-sized law firm with a turnover of approximately 100 million had to produce a communications document to explain a class action, which they were leading on, to members of the general public. They wished to persuade a certain group of the public, who had been affected by the issue, to join the class action. The first draft of the document, which had been put

"It makes little sense to take an expensive fee earner away from income-generating client work in order to do a poor writing job, rather than letting someone who is highly skilled at writing do the work for you at what is likely to be a fraction of the cost."

together by solicitors and barristers, was not comprehensible to a member of the public. Wisely, they had realised the problem and passed the document to a communication specialist for an opinion. They rewrote the document, made it easy to read, persuasive and fit for purpose. It was also reduced in length from approximately 20 pages to three, ensuring that it would be more likely to be read.

The final stage is to pay attention to proofreading and detail. This includes spellings, grammar, layout and typing consistency, and important points such as the spelling of client names and company names. There is a proliferation of unusual company names in the current business market and these are often spelled wrong, or should appear as one word and are split into two accidentally. The spellchecker on your computer can be your worst enemy; how many of us have experienced instances when completely inappropriate words have replaced our original typing? The last place you want this to happen is in a target client's proposal documents!

16. Visuals and design

Good visual presentation will greatly enhance the finished product. Attempting to fiddle around in PowerPoint or some other computer

"Never stop pitching. There is always something more you can do. It will impress your client and take you that one step ahead of your competition."

program rarely creates an impressive end result. Plain text from Word or a similar package does not give you the option to enhance your tone, theme and key messages. The visual impression is as powerful as the content. Remember the employment lawyer who saw how similar all the documents were on the in-house lawyer's desk? If his had had good visual design, it would have stood a better chance of attracting attention or being memorable.

Visual design, colour and layout can create mood and tone. You may have your own brand guidelines, selected fonts and proposal document design that have been produced by a marketing department. A good professional designer will be able to incorporate these key brand design elements, while introducing components that reflect your client's brand and your selected tone and theme. You may also want to introduce graphics and pictures, depending on your target clients' personalities. A designer will help you to select these or create the graphics you are after. Their work is infinitely more impressive than anything we can create ourselves.

17. You think you are finished... then go the extra mile

Never stop pitching. There is always something more you can do. It will impress your client and take you that one step ahead of your competition.

> "We were aware that we were up against some very tough competition for a big contract and we also knew there were a number of factors that were not in our favour. Once the RFP response had been completed, we knew we needed to go that one step further. After a short brainstorming session, we decided to add a completely new dimension to our submission. After all, submissions are now electronic, which gives a great opportunity to create something new. The business we were pitching to rented out recreational vehicles and hire cars in a number of different countries. The younger members of our team suggested, as they were the company's target market, that they should experience one of the RVs and a couple of the others should hire a car. They filmed their experiences on their mobile phones. We also filmed a brainstorming session. The whole team were sitting in the office, surrounded by pictures and research about the client, pinned up on the walls. The film demonstrated the effort we had gone to and how much we had tried to understand the client, and showed us as human beings rather than a list of names on a piece of paper. We also included a personal message from our managing partner, who was dressed in a similar style to their staff. The films included our tone, theme and key messages for the pitch. We shot straight into the last two firms and were invited to present personally."

18. Getting in front of the client

The result we want from all this work is to find ourselves in front of a target client who is already feeling engaged and interested in what we might contribute to the business. We may have been asked to present or it may be a one-to-one meeting with a new contact. The point is that they are already interested enough to have asked us through the door.

If you have done your preparation and followed the method above, you should be feeling confident and ready to have the conversation. All your bases are covered and you know the key messages, evidence and motivational points that are relevant for the personalities in the room.

Being confident is more than half the battle. Any pitching situation, by its very nature, involves elements of stress and pressure. In a highly competitive marketplace, the pressure to win work can be overbearing. We feel pressure not only from competitors, but also from other partners and the management committee within our firm. We have targets. It is a buyer's market and clients know that. We know that. By following this process in the run-up to a meeting or pitch, you should have greater confidence in your ability to win and have the edge over any potential competition, which will shine through during the meeting. You will speak and act more confidently; and if you are correct in your analysis of the business and the people, you will quickly see a response in the tone and feedback from the client. This positive reinforcement bouncing from you to your client and back will create a productive environment for doing business.

19. Face to face

In advance of any contact session, you may want to ask the target whether there is anything particular they want to get out of the meeting. This will help you to establish what the basis of the meeting is in their mind and allow you to prepare appropriately. It may also encourage them to focus and think about whether there is anything you could potentially work on with them.

Initially, it is a good idea to talk about your basic credentials and who you are. It is best to give a short, sharp summary of them. It is always a good idea to have practised this on someone else first, to make sure you hit the key points clearly. You cannot assume that your target will have read anything about you or your work beforehand.

> "If you pitch to us, we want you to tell us about innovation. Demonstrate to us your expertise through examples and illustrations. Show it rather than say it. People love stories. They are emotionally based, connective and they bring happiness. Stories are how big brands motivate you to spend a lot of money on a product. Lawyers can do the same. The

> outcome of the story can show the unique qualities that you will bring to the table."

In face-to-face meetings, the temptation is to fall into the trap of listing all the things that we have done or are doing in order to demonstrate our expertise. A more powerful and persuasive approach is to simply share examples as part of an interactive conversation. Ask the client how their business is going and whether there are other challenges that they are facing. You are letting them talk about themselves, so they feel listened to and understood. For example, your client may speak about a certain problem they have. You can express your concern and understanding of the difficulties they must be facing, and then say how it reminds you of a situation you had with client X. You can explain how you dealt with it.

20. The presentation

If you have been asked to present to the client, it probably means that you have made it successfully through an RFP response stage. You have therefore been judged to have all the necessary technical skills, relevant experience and suitable credentials; but so have your competitors that have also made it through. It may be that you've been asked to present because you have come up with innovative ideas and suggestions that appeal to the client, and they want to hear more from you and allow the team to meet you too. Whatever the situation, from this point on, your experience, credentials and technical ability are no longer the strengths in your case. Now you have to demonstrate what else you can bring to the table and what value you can give to the client over and above these basics. This is where all the work in your preparation process will pay off, in terms of your understanding of the client and ability to respond to their needs.

For some, the prospect of having to do a formal presentation as part of a pitch is nerve wracking, whereas others relish the opportunity of performing to a group. Both approaches can lead to problems in terms of delivery. Being nervous and underestimating yourself can mean that you do not show yourself to your best. If you are too confident, you can underestimate the amount of time that needs to go into the preparation in order to make the presentation completely client-centric. Sometimes being far too confident with the client can put the client off. It's all about responding to their needs.

The solution to the potential problems with both approaches is: rehearse, rehearse, rehearse. Once again, it is a good idea if someone unconnected with the pitch listens to your presentation. They will be able to give you an honest analysis of the content and tell you whether it all makes sense, whether the logic flows in the argument and whether it is centred on the client and comes across well.

"One of the biggest issues that businesses raise about pitches is that they meet someone who is good at performing during the meeting, but who has little to do with the account going forward. They then find themselves working with completely different people."

> "It's no good just bringing the rainmaker out for the pitch meeting. We want to know that you work as a team. We once had a situation where a very slick, confident partner turned up to present. He shook hands with the others from his own firm, as none of them knew each other. It absolutely killed their chances."

Remembering the mantra "What's in it for the client?" will not only guide you in structuring the presentation around the client, but also make you think about each and every point that you include in a different way.

For example, you could say, "Our employment lawyers have extensive experience in dealing with factory and warehouse workers." Or instead, you could say, "We understand that many of your staff issues arise in the factory and the warehouse. These sorts of issues can be very hard to handle for employers. We have dealt with many similar cases for other clients and have advised them take action that reduces the number of problems that they experience. For example, a few months ago, we encountered..." By engaging them in another client example, you have captured their interest through a storytelling technique. People always want to know what happens next! It also demonstrates that you are 'doers', not 'talkers'.

In terms of building a team for the presentation, it is essential that you take all the people that will be working on the account. One of the biggest issues that businesses raise about pitches is that they meet someone who is good at performing during the meeting, but who has little to do with the account going forward. They then find themselves working with completely different people. The other problem they encounter is that senior lawyers attend the meeting, but more junior staff run the account on a day-to-day basis. However, none of the junior staff are invited to attend the presentation. Clients want to meet the people they will be working with. They want to establish whether they could have a good relationship with those people.

> During one very competitive pitch, the team had managed to get down to the last two and both were being given the opportunity to present. The presentation went brilliantly and feedback was excellent. The client said that it was lively, focused on their problems, engaging and impressive in terms of technical ideas; and yet they did not give them the work. The client said that it was a very hard decision. The reason they chose the winning firm was because it had brought the entire team that would be working on the account to the presentation, whereas the other firm had not. The client said they had wanted to know whether they could build a relationship with all the people they would be working with.

A presentation need not be a one-way stream of information. You can give your clients plenty of opportunity to ask questions, to input ideas and to engage in discussing the work with you. Once they begin to discuss it, they will subconsciously begin to see how you would work together as a team. They will start to feel a bond with you and a sense of ownership of mutual projects.

It is always interesting to see whether the client begins to use the word 'we' to address you during the discussion. This is an excellent indicator that all is going well. It is also possible to use the word 'we' during your presentation to indicate you and the client. This creates a subconscious bond with the client, encouraging them to focus on the project and its success rather than on judging whether you are the right person. It is important to judge the right moment during the presentation to begin to use the word 'we'. If it is used too early, it can make the client uncomfortable.

Visual aids can be very poor in presentations. We have all suffered 'death by PowerPoint'. The problem is that people use visual aids so they can be handouts after the presentation. That is not a visual aid. It is a handout and should not be put up on the big screen. Visuals are also used as a replacement for a script, again making them text dense, unreadable and a distraction from the speaker. You want people to be concentrating on what you are saying, not reading the overheads instead. Visual aids are exactly that. They are an 'aid' to enhance your message, not a replacement for you or what you are saying. The best slides have perhaps one or two short lines of text and then clever pictures or useful graphics. They should add an extra dimension to what you are saying, not take from it.

> "For a multinational business, we produced a document that could be handed out afterwards, but then produced a completely different presentation that contained the same messages. It relied on small amounts of texts, visual examples, photos and graphics. We had it professionally designed and the client commented that the presentation was refreshingly different and was much more interesting."

21. Feedback

Never be afraid of feedback. Nobody ever likes to hear anything negative about themselves and we fear what others might say. Generally, lawyers are far more critical of themselves than business people are of them! Always ask for feedback, whether you have had a one-to-one meeting, been asked for a proposal document or done a

"If you walk away not knowing why a decision has been made, you do not give yourself the opportunity to improve what you do, to learn from your mistakes or to appreciate where you are making an excellent impact on potential clients."

formal presentation. If you walk away not knowing why a decision has been made, you do not give yourself the opportunity to improve what you do, to learn from your mistakes or to appreciate where you are making an excellent impact on potential clients. Pitching is a learning process. The more we do, the more we learn and the better we get. Try to see it objectively, do not take it personally and, most importantly, do not blame members of the team if mistakes have been made. Pitching is most successful when it is done in a positive and encouraging environment. It is a long-term activity and investment needs to be made in positive learning and development for the whole team.

Figure 1. Approaching a pitch

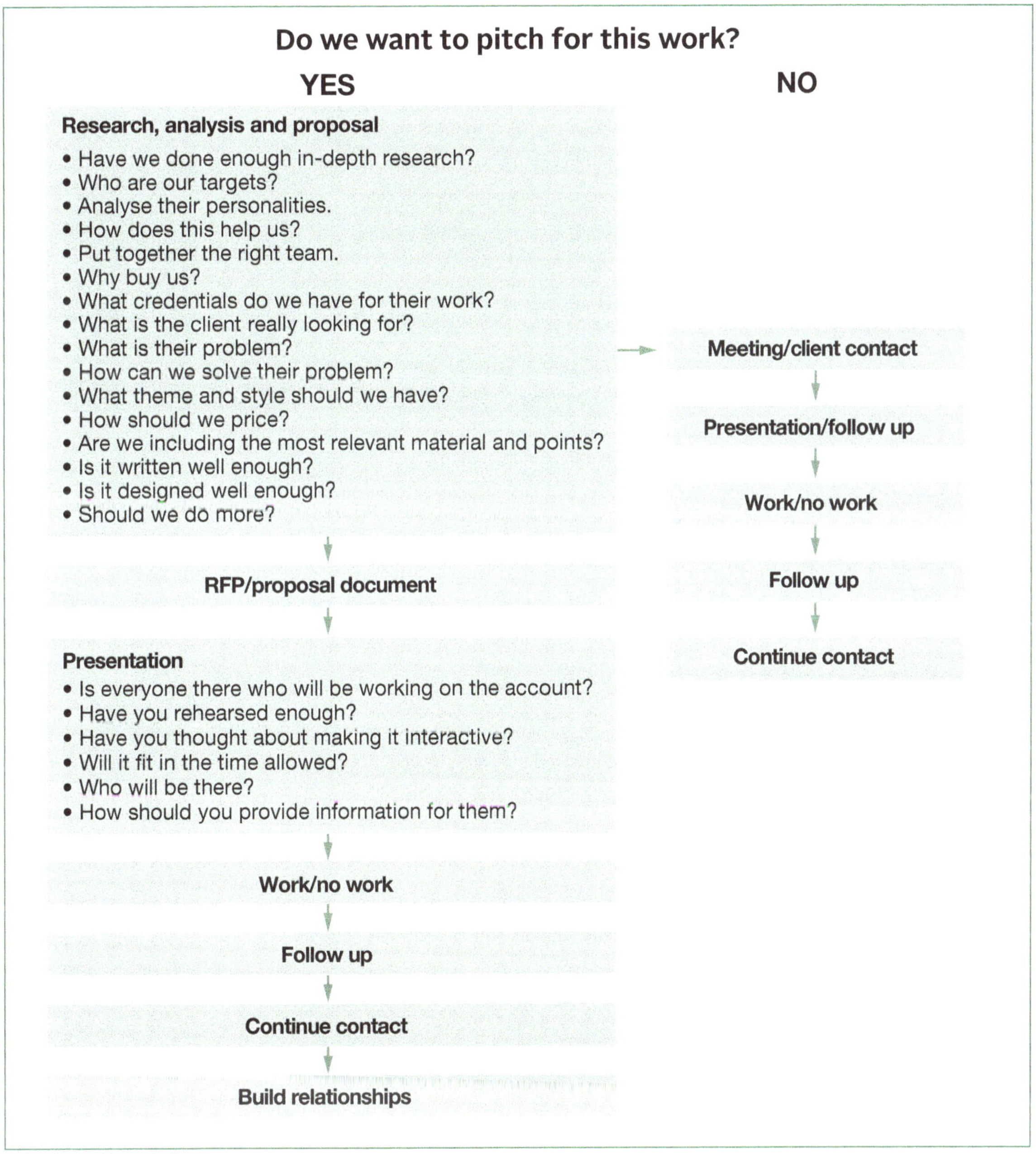

You can help the client if you are constructive in the feedback you ask them for. Ask them to assess:

- the content;
- the work that you proposed;
- the pricing model;
- the style and presentation;
- whether they could they see where your firm offered something different from other firms; and
- why they made the decision they did.

"We had been assured that they were looking for somebody who could deliver the work better than their current law firm. When it came down to it, we realised they had made a decision on based on price and that was the driving factor. It was very annoying, as we had not focused on the area as we did not see it as a priority. But when we looked back at the conversations we had had with the client, we realised that they had mentioned price a lot. We had made the mistake of believing what they said on the surface and not thinking a bit more deeply about it. Clients are not always honest."

22. Now go and do it!

There is only one thing left now, and that is for you to go out there and give some of these new ideas a go. We have looked at:

- creating a positive context for you as a foundation to winning work;
- the common mistakes that business sees when legal firms try to win work; and
- a methodology for pitching that should give you and your team more confidence, a more thorough approach and better insight into the real motivations of your target clients.

Do not expect yourself to be perfect at it the first time you try this new method. You will strengthen and improve your approach over time and gain confidence by seeing the positive changes in response that you will get from clients by trying it.

Remember that no one is born with these skills; they must be learned and developed over time. This means that you can improve and are perfectly capable of competing with the best in the marketplace. Business does not necessarily want the most amazing presenter, the most confident speaker or the most brilliant writer. Their secret is that they want someone who thinks about them, all the time. So, make sure that's you!

About the author

Rebecca Harding
Marketing and business development specialist, Saltwhistle Communications
rebecca@saltwhistle.com

Rebecca Harding is a marketing and business development specialist. She is the worldwide chairman of the Society of Women Writers and Journalists and was recently awarded Highly Commended Finalist in the UK Institute of Director's 'Non Executive Director of the Year'. She is a professional member of the Chartered Institute of Public Relations and is a retired vice chairman of the Chartered Institute of Marketing.

Ms Harding founded Saltwhistle Communications in 2000 and has developed a portfolio of clients within the professional services industry. Clients have ranged from multinational firms such as accountants Deloitte, PwC and EY to law firms such as Stephenson Harwood, Norton Rose Fulbright and Weightmans, as well as international businesses such as WPP's Mediacom, J Walter Thompson (now Wunderman Thompson) and Mindshare.
Each client benefits from a range of services, including practice/business consultancy, partner and board advisory services, marketing, pitching and business development, innovation workshops and communications solutions. Much of Ms Harding's current work is international and she works with firms to increase their international effectiveness, as well as helping draw together their international tenders/pitches.

Prior to establishing Saltwhistle Communications, Ms Harding was responsible for communications at Andersens. She also worked in marketing within the energy industry, with corporations such as BNFL, BP, ESSO and Shell.

Ms Harding was an elected politician. As a UK county councillor, she oversaw the Education and Young People brief, and was on the parliamentary list. She has held a range of positions, including being a member of the Institute of Chartered Accountants in England and Wales' Future of Practice Committee and a member of the Small Business Advisory Panel at the ACCA.

She is currently involved in a chat show for the BBC and has been quoted and published widely in trade journals, as well as national newspapers such as the *Sunday Times*.

In her spare time, Ms Harding has qualified as a yacht skipper and has trained as a game ranger in the Kruger, and as a falconer.

About Globe Law and Business

Globe Law and Business was established in 2005, and from the very beginning, we set out to create law books which are sufficiently high level to be of real use to the experienced professional, yet still accessible and easy to navigate. Most of our authors are drawn from Magic Circle and other top commercial firms, both in the UK and internationally.

Our titles are carefully produced, with the utmost attention paid to editorial, design and production processes. We hope this results in high-quality books which are easy to read, and a pleasure to own. All our new books are also available as ebooks, which are compatible with most desktop, laptop and tablet devices.

We have recently expanded our portfolio to include a new range of journals, Special Reports and Good Practice Guides, available both digitally and in hard copy format, and produced to the same high standards as our books.

We'd very much like to hear from you with your thoughts and ideas for improving what we offer. Please do feel free to email me at sian@globelawandbusiness.com with your views.

Sian O'Neill, managing director

www.ingramcontent.com/pod-product-compliance
Ingram Content Group UK Ltd.
Pitfield, Milton Keynes, MK11 3LW, UK
UKHW060219140526
471061UK00005B/42

9 781787 422742